lasgow Life and its service brands, including Glasgow
braries, (found at www.glasgowlife.org.uk) are operating
ames for Culture and Sport Glasgow.

**Glasgow**
CITY COUNCIL

# BLUFFOCRACY

PROVOCATIONS

# BLUFFOCRACY

## JAMES BALL AND ANDREW GREENWAY

SERIES EDITOR:

YASMIN ALIBHAI-BROWN

Biteback Publishing

First published in Great Britain in 2018 by
Biteback Publishing Ltd
Westminster Tower
3 Albert Embankment
London SE1 7SP
Copyright © James Ball and Andrew Greenway 2018

ISBN 978-1-78590-411-0

10 9 8 7 6 5 4 3 2 1

A CIP catalogue record for this book is available from the British Library.

Set in Stempel Garamond

Printed and bound in Great Britain by
CPI Group (UK) Ltd, Croydon CR0 4YY

# Contents

# Introduction

I T'S TWENTY-FIVE PAST nine on Wednesday
morning in early December, and a sleepy-looking
Brexit Secretary is about to face off with MPs.
At stake are the contents of a series of reports whose
existence has been disputed for months: about how different Brexit scenarios will affect fifty-eight different
industries, a matter of serious policy detail with huge
repercussions for the UK economy.

David Davis was before MPs on the Brexit Select
Committee, the forum by which ministers are supposed
to be held to account for their decisions. But this con-
frontation, and the months of wrangling that led to it,
had virtually nothing to do with the impact of the government's policy.

Instead, for months, Davis, MPs and journalists had

wrangled over semantics. A year before, he had assured MPs his department was carrying out 'fifty-seven sets of analyses' on Brexit. Months later, a junior Brexit minister repeated that the government had 'conducted analysis of over fifty sectors of the economy'. By October 2017, Davis had promised MPs that the impact assessments not only existed but went into 'excruciating detail' – and said the Prime Minister would know the 'summary outcomes' of them.

But that excruciating detail was apparently not for MPs or the public to see. Instead, a merry dance played out over months of newspaper editorials before the Speaker ordered the release of the documents. For the first, and perhaps only, time, people got very excited about whether or not an 'impact assessment' was the same thing as a 'sectoral analysis'. And when the supposedly detailed documents were finally released, there were just 850 pages to cover all fifty-eight reports – around fifteen pages per sector – much of it apparently hastily thrown together by civil servants at a level described by one MP as 'Wikipedia-lite'.

Davis's showdown over the year-long wrangle had

nothing to do with the contents of the documents, and consequently nothing to do with the long-term effects of one of the biggest decisions any British government has made in decades. Davis made sure of that: he made sure he hadn't read any of the 850 pages before appearing before the committee. 'For absolute, complete transparency on it, I was provided with a sample of two of the chapters in the week before they were given to the Committee,' he told MPs. 'I did not read them deliberately; I took the view that I wanted to be able to say that I did not read them.'

After little more than an hour of uneven and partisan questioning, Davis left the committee, citing another commitment – despite having been warned by the Speaker that Parliament should be his top priority. The dénouement of a year's wrangling over the impact of Brexit ended with an hour's discussion of who read what and when, and whether 'impact assessments' and 'sectoral analyses' are different things. Davis himself left unscathed.

That year-long impact assessment fight is emblematic of three of the institutions that shape British public life. Politics, the civil service and the media are – with honourable exceptions – run by people who are bluffing, winging it, obsessed with process over substance, and dominated by short-termism.

The tops of these institutions are dominated by men – it is still predominantly men – whose primary skills are most often talking well, writing well and quickly mastering just enough detail of a brief to get by. We live in a country where George Osborne can become a newspaper editor despite never having worked in news, squeezing it in alongside five other jobs; where a columnist can go from calling a foreign head of state a 'wanker' to being Foreign Secretary in six months; where the minister who holds on to his role for eighteen months has more experience on the job than the supposedly permanent senior civil servants.

These values aren't just cultural: they're baked into how our elites are educated, how career advancement works and how people get noticed. This approach ranges from top-flight entrants to the civil service being required to take on four different roles in two years, to the UK Cabinet needing to be hired from the ranks of

MPs, who rarely have specialist experience in the departments they lead.

This book aims to chronicle how Britain became a bluffocracy – and what real-world consequences it has for us all, from frustrating scrutiny, to stymieing diversity, to contributing to the short-termism that fuels many of the country's political failures and scandals.

✻ ✻ ✻

The UK's preoccupation with the jack of all trades long predates any 21st-century government – it is in many ways an outgrowth of the Victorian concept of the 'gentleman amateur', the nobleman who can turn his hand with great ability to any one of dozens of fields, whether in public life, the sciences or sport. One of the pinnacles of the concept was Sir Francis Galton – a true polymath born to wealth, with more than 300 academic papers to his name. Galton was the discoverer of the concept of correlation, one of the first meteorologists, and the first proponent of the morally dubious concept of eugenics. But most of us are not Galton: we may be good at one or two things, but even then it takes years to become an expert.

Expecting anyone, however smart, to master many different fields is a recipe for failure – but it is also the basic requirement for ministers, journalists and senior civil servants. Whatever he may think, Michael Gove is not this generation's Galton – yet, like many other ministers, he has so far been called upon as an expert in the UK's education system, justice system and, most recently, environmental and rural affairs.

The difficulties of expecting ministers to be the master of so many fields was perhaps best highlighted when Gove appeared before MPs and was asked whether he could manage his stated target. 'If "good" requires pupil performance to exceed the national average, and if all schools must be good, how is this mathematically possible?' the English graduate was asked at committee in 2012. 'By getting better all the time,' he replied, prompting the question of whether he was 'better at literacy than numeracy' at school. Gove could not recall.

Expecting GCSE-level maths from the Education Secretary should not sound unreasonable, but the British establishment has a long-held suspicion of installing experts at the highest level. Sir Winston Churchill, regarded by many as one of the country's finest Prime Ministers, famously said that scientists should be 'on tap, not on top' – an attitude still built into many institutions to this day, deliberately or otherwise.

The UK is facing a new array of global challenges that rely on specialist knowledge, from the rise of AI, to working out solutions to climate change, to tackling cybercrime and the lurch into the internet era. And yet science and technology remain marginalised in three of the country's key institutions.

Research by Nesta suggests only 9 per cent of candidates at the 2017 general election had degrees in science or technology. Around 60 per cent of applicants to the civil service had degrees in humanities, social sciences or languages – versus less than 15 per cent from a science background. In journalism, the effect is even more stark, where research by the Reuters Institute for the Study of Journalism found that only 3 per cent of journalists said they had a specialism in science or technology. By contrast, 47 per cent said they weren't a specialist in anything.

The values of all three institutions tend to reward people willing to change beats and move around, again rewarding generalists over specialists – but also encouraging a short-termism in reporting and policy-making alike. In government, this is what encourages ministers and the civil servants who support them to focus on making new policies, knowing they likely won't be around when any consequences come home to roost – as the government learned the hard way in the spring of 2018 with the Windrush scandal. Brexit may end up being the biggest Pandora's box of all.

Rewarding this narrow range of traits hurts diversity – which means a smaller range of voices representing British public debate and shaping the rules that govern the nation. If politics and the media are overwhelmingly white, male and middle-class, then the views and experience of people who aren't in that group are missing from the debate – with negative consequences for them, and for all of us.

Only around 40 per cent of the top of the civil service is made up of women, while fewer than one in three MPs is female. In journalism, men are around 50 per cent more likely than women to earn over £48k a year – a proxy for senior roles in a profession with a more fluid structure than most. People from ethnic minorities make up only around 7 per cent of the top of the civil service (versus around 15 per cent of the population); they also make up 8 per cent of MPs and 6 per cent of national journalists. The skills and the backgrounds prized by these professions sustain these trends – and favour those with private educations, too.

Amid a huge public debate around curbing immigration, the UK has a long list of occupations with skills shortages – roles that we find it hard to fill based on people already living in the UK, suggesting we struggle to train up people in those fields. Again and again those roles are specialist and usually technical, from nuclear industry programme managers, to physical scientists, to virtually every type of engineer, to IT managers and numerous medical roles. Perhaps if these professions were more represented in policy-making and reporting, we would have better ideas on how to fill the vacancies – or at the very least a more urgent sense of the shortages and their consequences.

Just because these things are long-running doesn't mean they're unchangeable: our institutions have gone through seismic changes in the past few decades, and have managed them. Newspapers are undergoing a shift from being distributed once a day via vans to a few hundred thousand people, to being spread on the internet in real time to millions – but for far less money. The civil service has faced upheaval after upheaval, as has Parliament. With effort, we could choose to value different things, changing who gets promoted and broadening the range of skills and personalities in public life. This isn't about getting rid of every jack of all trades – it's just about making them a smaller part of the mix.

First, though, we'll try to convince you of why we think there's a problem – and part of that involves a confession: we've both been part of it. James Ball and Andrew Greenway (that's us) are both graduates in Philosophy, Politics and Economics,[1] perhaps the ultimate bluffer's degree. Worse still, we both studied it at the University of Oxford, at the same time. Andrew

---

[1] And are both unbearable enough to write about themselves in the third person.

graduated with a first-class degree, which explains his subsequent career in the civil service, where he entered the senior ranks of the service at twenty-seven, before leaving a few years later to go freelance. James got a mediocre second-class degree, which explains his entry into journalism.

If, when it comes to bluffers, it takes one to know one, we have a good claim to knowledge. We've tried to set out ahead how generalists – or bluffers – are trained, then how and why they rise in the professions we've mentioned, and then set out more fully the consequences of that. Most sentences are from both of us, but occasionally we'll insert an aside from one or the other of us *(Like this – James)*.

We think Britain hasn't so much 'had enough of experts'; it's just had enough of the fake experts it sees daily. Trying to learn how to respect experts and build their work into public life would be a big challenge – but none of our organisations exist in a vacuum, and so we think building any kind of real change will have to look at how so many of the people at the top are educated as it stands, and the values and skills that education instils.

Part

# Part I

# Becoming a bluffer

**A**FEW LUCKY BLUFFERS are born. Most are made.

Back in the day, responsibility for the moulding process fell largely to the private school system. What centuries of upper-class family conditioning began, Eton, Harrow and the rest would finish off. Schools literally whipped a fresh batch of British aristocracy into shape, inculcating ideals that would stick for life.

The private schools continue to prosper today, but the rise of the middle classes has shifted the focus further up the education chain. These days, the bluffer's finishing school is at university – and at one Oxford course in particular.

Philosophy, Politics and Economics – PPE – is the

ultimate vocational course for the bluffer in waiting.
From its earliest days, PPE has been the golden ticket
into Britain's political, media and institutional elites.
More than that, it has shaped the way those elites operate, the very machinery of the state, and our beliefs
about how intellect, expertise and knowledge intersect.
For that reason, it's worth dissecting at some length –
to understand how people who go on to positions of
power are shaped by their education.

PPE was first offered by Oxford in 1920. As is typical
for British institutions, this move was made in response
to a threat, rather than proactively grasping an opportu-
nity. Dons were worried about being squeezed out by
a combination of newcomers like LSE and Manches-
ter, and the old enemy Cambridge, whose newfangled
economics course was proving popular. Money, prestige and influence were at risk.

The university was keen to reassert its position as
the destination of choice for the people going on to
run the country. Oxford's Classics degree[2] had long

---

2   Known variously as Greats, Classics or Literae Humaniores. Classics remains
    a popular Oxford course. It seems to spawn an unhealthy number of lawyers.

been the default option, giving future leaders a firm grounding in the greatest hits of Greek and Latin, plus a heavy dose of philosophy. An unwillingness to devalue Classics shaped much of Oxford's hesitancy.

However, rumblings had been growing as to whether Classics really served as ideal academic preparation for Britain's post-Victorian administration. Many thought that civil servants needed something more up to date to deal with the challenges emerging from the First World War's aftermath. Oxford scrambled to find answers. An undergraduate degree in Civil Service was drawn up, but then dropped. PPE stepped into the gap. It really shouldn't be seen as a surprise that PPE has become the establishment's degree course of choice; this is precisely what it was designed to be.

Not everyone was delighted by the new course. Oxford's philosophers were particularly aggrieved, viewing it (rightly) as diminishing the central role their subject had enjoyed in Classics. They were bought off by making Philosophy the first P of PPE. Other objections were harder to dismiss. Members of the old guard decried PPE as 'a soft option for the weaker man'.

Today, the university is unabashed in its pride in PPE, playing up how exactly important it believes it is. In explaining why someone would choose to take the course, Oxford claims PPE was 'born of the conviction that study of the great modern works of social, political and philosophical thought could have a transformative effect on students' intellectual lives, and thereby on society at large'.

They have a right to be pleased, because PPE was ultimately successful in its aim. It shored up Oxford's role as lead provider of the country's political elite. A generation on from PPE's creation, Oxford has dominated 10 Downing Street. Ten post-war Prime Ministers have an Oxford degree on their CV.[3] Britain has had more PPE Prime Ministers than female Prime Ministers. Meanwhile, Classics remained as an option to cater for traditionalists; five post-war Cabinet Secretaries (heads of the civil service) have stuck with the old favourite.

If PPE were a private members' club rather than a

---

3    Of the other four to have the job since 1945, one went to Edinburgh (Gordon Brown) and the remaining three did not go to university (John Major, James Callaghan and Winston Churchill).

harmless university course, its roster might get a lot more scrutiny. The PPE club includes at least ten former Prime Ministers from outside the UK, several Presidents, and around a hundred British Cabinet ministers. Rupert Murdoch, Nick Robinson, Stephanie Flanders and Robert Peston are among the hundreds more alumni now in the senior media ranks. At the time of writing, at least three Permanent Secretaries had studied PPE, including Brexit supremo Oliver Robbins. So did Aung San Suu Kyi. So did Toby Young. So, at the time of writing, is Malala Yousafzai.

So, if PPE is a course designed to create leaders, what does it actually teach you? As anyone with a chance of getting on the road to blagging would intuit, the first step to understanding that is to find a dangerously abridged account of the main points, then consider yourself ready to pile in. We're here to help. Forget about getting an MBA in twelve months; here's how to get PPE in thirty minutes.

Before we get started, there's the small matter of getting onto the course in the first place. This is not easy. Less than 15 per cent of prospective PPE students receive an offer from Oxford. In 2016, no Oxford course received more applicants. If you beat the UCAS form numbers game, you're then into the interview process.

Oxbridge interviews have a reputation for asking odd questions: 'How do you know you are really present for this interview?' and other such posers. This has turned into an annual ritual where newspapers will write rubbish features on the mad inquests set by tutors. Admittedly, these topics rarely come up in the pub.[4] But the questions aren't the real test. The real test is the scenario: how well does a teenager cope with walking into a grand room infused with centuries of intellectual history and being asked questions designed to knock them off balance? If they are calm, plausible and relatively coherent in their response, the omens are good. They belong. They're either brilliant or they can blag.

Now you've arrived, it's worth taking stock of what you've actually signed up for. It may not be exactly what you expect.

For example, as a student of Philosophy, Politics and

---

4   Except in Oxbridge, where, unfortunately, they often come up in the pub.

Economics, you might expect to be spending the next three years of your life becoming proficient in... well, philosophy, politics and economics. Surprisingly, this is often not the case.

After your first year, which concludes with a few short pass-or-fail papers in each subject, you can kiss goodbye to one of the disciplines for ever. All PPEists leave Oxford with gaping blind spots in their understanding. PPE allows people to claim a first-class degree strongly implying a firm command of economics having only had to prove once, two years before graduating, that they can count on their fingers.

Of all the possible university courses to condense into a ridiculously short space of time, PPE seems like one of the least likely to work. There are few other undergraduate options within the British university system that offer up so much choice. There are more than sixty papers to choose from and a syllabus spanning several millennia of deep thinkers. How can you possibly distil all of that into capsule form?

It's worth getting used to the idea, because there's a lot of cramming ahead. PPE offers the ultimate exam anxiety experience. Your three years of toil are eventually judged by your performance in eight three-hour papers taken at the end of your third Oxford summer. Twenty-four hours under exam conditions will make or break your degree.[5] Squashing big problems into small chunks of knowledge that can be spat out again is what you do now.

The good news is that there's one task we can dismiss from our half-hour primer: how to make links between different papers. Why? Because real PPE students don't have to either. Despite impressions, PPE isn't a multidisciplinary degree in the truest sense; it's a jumble of unconnected puzzle pieces taken from the three disciplines. It is left up to students to assemble those parts into something meaningful if they wish. Some do. Most don't, because making an effort at synthesis isn't something that PPE's examiners ask for – other than the optional dissertation, there's no mechanism in the

---

5    There's a small caveat to this: PPE students can choose to substitute a 15,000-word thesis in one of the three disciplines for one of the eight papers. Those who do – usually around a sixth of the people in each intake – only have to worry about exams for 87.5 per cent of their total mark.

degree to reward trying to connect its seemingly unrelated strands. That's left to the student's own discretion.

On closer examination, PPE is not quite as broad or obscure as it looks. Every student sitting final exams must take at least four of just thirteen 'core' papers across the three disciplines. Learn enough to cover all those bases, and you're well on track to grasping PPE. The only problem with that strategy is that those thirteen papers cover subjects with a very expansive sweep.

If we're keeping to our thirty-minute target, that leaves two minutes for an introduction and some conclusions, and a couple of minutes each on topics like Microeconomics, Knowledge and Reality, and International Relations. Even PPEists would baulk at attempting to get a firm grip on all of Ethics and Quantitative Economics in the time it takes to boil an egg.

Luckily for us, when it comes to getting a PPE degree, the content isn't really what counts. When you enter the real world, nobody cares what papers you studied as a PPE undergraduate. It's methods that matter. The conditions in which students go about learning are essentially the same for almost every topic PPE throws at them.

Learn how to do it once, and you can make a reasonable go at tackling pretty much any topic.

*  *  *

Tutorials – and, depending on subject choice, a small number of seminars – are the only mandatory classes a PPE student will take during their three-year degree. It is a PPE student's prerogative as to whether they spend well over 95 per cent of their time at Oxford sleeping, getting involved in student societies, pretending that rowing is fun, or simply lying about in a chair eating crisps. PPE didn't even bother with putting on undergraduate lectures until the 1960s, and attendance is still entirely optional. This means that all but two to three hours of each week are theoretically left to self-directed study: tutorials are showtime.

Most of what follows relates mainly to philosophy and politics tutorials: in economics, class sizes are a little larger and the tutorial proceeds more like a regular lesson. It's easier to be caught out if you can't, for example, draw a basic graph that was supposed to be at the core of the week's study. This may be why PPE students who focused on economics tend to have a marginally firmer attachment to knowing things before coming to an opinion; alternatively, it may be that their self-denial just runs much deeper.

Anyway, in philosophy and politics, the tutorial format is one which will be largely unfamiliar to anyone who didn't attend Oxford or Cambridge. Two or three students will go to the study of their tutor (very occasionally a student is tutored one-on-one), having each prepared an essay over the previous week, which will have been issued alongside a recommended reading list.

The mission for the student is then to get through the next sixty minutes without embarrassing yourself – or, if you're more diligent than average, trying to demonstrate competence to your tutor. Often the set-up is that one student (taking it in turns week by week) will be asked to read their essay aloud, and the other student(s) will be asked to critique it, with the tutor jumping in to provoke new questions or challenges.

The format is initially intimidating, but over time usually approaches something close to being enjoyable.

Building experience in PPE, like getting better at blagging, is a case of learning to enjoy the game for its own sake, rather than any higher outcome. When it comes to the tutorial game, a student quickly learns that if it isn't their week to read, the best way to get through is to savage a tutorial partner's essay. If you can come up with enough niggling counterarguments to prolong the discussion, your under-baked work might escape anything but the most cursory scrutiny.

On the other hand, if it's your week to read your essay, you learn to be most provocative on the material you've read the most extensively, to try to draw the discussion towards your strongest ground. If you're feeling especially sneaky, you may even base the lion's share of your argument on an obscure book that wasn't on the reading list. There's no chance your tutorial partner will have read it and, if you're lucky, it might put the tutor on the back foot as well. This is a risky strategy, however, because it relies on (a) you having actually understood the obscure book, and (b) that book not having been written by a close friend of the tutor, unbeknownst to you.

The snag for many students is that even if you have done extensive reading and prepared a good essay, your tutorial partner's essay may come from an entirely different direction – they've played the old 'random book' trick on you, or simply approached the matter from another angle. Even when you've done the work, you will have to think very rapidly on your feet to come up with a reasonable response to their essay, and your preparation will be largely irrelevant. In other words, doing the work properly doesn't necessarily make you more effective in tutorials if you don't know the tricks as well. If you just know the tricks, meanwhile, that will often get you most of the way to safety.

The strengths of this system are that it rewards quick thinking and strong reasoning. The weakness is that it fails to reward in-depth understanding, or those who think better on paper than in person. Given the one-week-on, one-week-off system, there is something of an incentive to feast following famine: if you're studying moral philosophy this term, you will tackle one (or more) of the world's great thinkers each week. If Immanuel Kant happened to be on the week you weren't reading, and you took advantage of that to whip off a quick half-thought-through essay, that's it – you may never encounter Kant or his categorical imperatives again throughout the course.[6]

There is also something deeply English about the punishment of a tutorial going wrong. Tutorials count for nothing towards your final mark, and your tutor will not set your exams. Perform badly, and they won't swear or shout. No, the punishment is embarrassment at having publicly lost the game. This is uncannily like British politics.

The tutorial system works well for high-flyer and disinterested student alike: the former is free to spend forty-plus hours each week working on polished essays and detailed notes to help with exam revision; the latter free to dash off an essay in a mad overnight scrabble – more on this later – and spend the rest of the week

---

6 A categorical imperative – not that you need to know this for the purposes of this book – is a moral obligation which applies in all circumstances, no matter what the outcome of it would be. So if there is a categorical imperative not to lie, and a murderer is looking for an innocent victim in your house, you shouldn't lie about the victim's location. Kant is pretty strict, really.

running for office in various student societies, making connections to help her later climb the greasy pole.

In a blog discussing Trevor Pateman's pamphlet 'The Poverty of PPE', the pained comments from tutors and students alike reflect this. In their view, PPE has become a case of 'churning it out: two essays a week, couple of days' reading for each, caffeine tablets, read it out to tutor, gone. Suits everybody, really: the not-bothered undergraduate and the tutor who wants to concentrate on the high-flyers.' What follows after Oxford is equally clear, as 'the right way to do this stuff is to spend three years getting snapshots, with the end aim of bullshitting some examiners, so as to go off and make loads of money'.

The direct effects of this system on encouraging blagging are clear, and their consequences are easy to see in public life: PPE students learn to argue and reason well, based on minimal actual knowledge. Getting through a high-stakes hour twice a week with preparation offering only partial help makes you a good debater and teaches you how to confidently present an argument with little to no knowledge of the field at hand. Anyone who's had a slippery colleague, or watched more than five minutes of Parliament, will have encountered the results of that talent. But the secondary effects of the tutorial system have their consequences too: when you need only perform for two hours a week, and you spend the remainder sleeping and eating crisps, it's easy to fall behind. This leads to PPE's most famous feature: the essay crisis.

*　　*　　*

David Cameron – at the time of writing, the UK's most recent PPE Prime Minister – was accused dozens of times, by political rivals, media outlets and academics alike, of running an 'essay crisis' government. What should be an obscure barb relating to one university degree has become a nationally known phrase, and represents a damning insult.

An essay crisis is a term heard in every university, but is especially familiar around those studying PPE: it's that feeling of having an impending deadline, usually early the following morning, and having done absolutely no work towards it. Perversely, it is a badge worn with pride. At the beginning of a classic essay crisis, the PPEist concerned has absolutely no knowledge whatsoever of the subject on which they must produce a thoughtful 2,000-word essay by the dawn. What follows is hours of panicked cramming, writing, adopting patented ways to stay awake *(I had a flatmate who swore by a cocktail of 50ml Benadryl plus three caffeine pills – JB)* and attempting to crib (a polite term for steal) notes from others.

There are numerous reasons these 'crises' happen more often in PPE than in other subjects, including the general attitude of PPEists and the fact that tutorials lend themselves to winging it, but the very structure of the course makes them inevitable for all but the most diligent and irritating students *(I didn't have essay crises. I used to do all my essays in the first six weeks of term, and take the last two weeks off. This made me as popular as you'd imagine – AG)*.

The structure of PPE at Oxford can easily set off a chain reaction of procrastination. Lectures are optional and therefore easily ignored, but they can be one of the keys to securing a top grade on the course for those playing the long game. This is because the lecture syllabus is set by the central university, the body who also sets the final exam paper. Knowing what is shaping their thinking is likely to prove helpful at crunch time.

However, in the short term, it is tutorials that represent the biggest concern for a PPE student. Their accompanying reading and essays are set by the college tutor giving them – who, while hopefully paying some regard to the overall course syllabus, is largely free to focus in on, and skip, whatever they like. That college tutor also sets a short exam called a 'collection' at the start of the following term, which has no effect on your final grade but is used by the college to keep tabs on you and make sure you're not falling too obviously behind. That means that, day to day and week by week, paying attention to lectures has far less benefit than just homing in on the things your tutor is interested in. Couple that with the fact that, as lectures play relatively little role in how Oxford academics are regarded by the university, they are of patchy quality (some are great, others decidedly less so), and they become very easy to miss. Final exams are two years away.

What student gets up for a 9 a.m. lecture if they don't need to?

The result is that at some point – whether through being distracted by social activities, getting a flurry of deadlines in a row, or simply being ill – a PPE student faces the prospect of a deadline twelve hours away, on a topic that came up in lectures but which they have never seen before. Your first essay crisis. This is a blessing in disguise, though, because once you've survived your first, you develop something of a strategy for how to produce a good essay with minimal knowledge, reading or time.

It goes a little something like this. The first step if you're producing an essay on a philosopher or political scientist's big idea is to not bother reading the original text. This will be long and dense, and you don't have that kind of time. Besides, far cleverer and better-prepared people than you have already devoted substantial parts of their career to poring over each word. The next step is to find them, looking through the reading list for critiques of the text which have been marked by the tutor as essential or most-useful reading, and skim as many as you can easily get hold of from the college library at midnight.[7]

From two or three of these critiques, the bulk of your essay comes together – you can now piece together a reasonable idea of what the original author was saying (and use the footnoted references to find a good page or two of their book to read, and take a quote or two from). Even better, there are now several different arguments against the original text at your disposal, one of which you should steal and build upon.

With one eye on tomorrow's tutorial, the final trick is to take the most obscure bit of reading on the list – or, even better, a paper that isn't on it – and find some argument or point within that to build into your essay. As well as helping deflect the worst of your tutorial partner's inquisitions, it suggests you've read more widely across the list. With a little bit of padding and good luck, this system delivers a 2,000-word essay that will comfortably see you through an Oxford tutorial in as little as four or five hours.

---

7   Many Oxford libraries never close. If they kept to normal working hours, a substantial minority of students would never read any books at all.

Therein lies the danger: once you've managed to do what is supposed to be twenty or so careful hours of reading, research and writing in less than a quarter of that time, it becomes your standard practice. If your essay crisis tutorial goes no worse than the usual set-piece, it feels irrational to revert to a more thoughtful approach. If it goes better than usual – and this often happens – it would surely be mad not to fall back on blagging next time.

This has numerous effects which stick with the essay crisis PPEist – a common trope, but not universal – through their subsequent careers. One is simply that with the huge amount of time freed up this way, PPEists have plenty of time to smooth their way through student society, building friendships, political alliances and strong extracurricular CVs to boost their way into the world of politics or the media. Another is the reinforcement of knowledge as another form of trickery – intellect being a quality that should run a mile wide, if only an inch deep.

The most dangerous, though, is the effect upon the ego of the individual concerned: after a good run of producing a convincing fake of twenty hours of work in just four, it's easy to believe that you can actually do in four hours what takes others twenty. It can create a dangerous sense of your own talent, and especially your own ability to bring everything together at the last minute. Most of life doesn't work like a PPE tutorial, though – as David Cameron found out to his peril decades after completing his degree.

Hang on, though. Why should it take so long for essay crisis merchants to get found out? Why isn't this form of glib knowledge caught out sooner, given the reputation of Oxford's exams for being rigorous and, notoriously, quite difficult?

\* \* \*

The final hurdle of university education at Oxford has always been a slightly unreal process. Centuries ago, degrees were awarded according to whether candidates could provide sensible answers to on-the-spot questions, sometimes asked while examiner and examinee proceeded through the city on horseback. These days,

PPE students are faced with a more conventional written paper.

Most PPE final exams have a similar look and feel. Candidates, dressed in the mandatory black suit, bow tie, gown and carnation[8] worn in the middle of the summer exam season's hottest weeks, sit down to a very thin exam paper, usually containing somewhere between ten and twenty different questions. From these, the candidate must choose three to answer in three hours. Economics papers might include more mathematics or graphs, but the challenge is the same.

The first quality that counts in PPE exams, therefore, is speed. Three hours might sound like a long time, but you have three essays to do. Most people write at about 10–20 words per minute; that's about three 1,000-word answers. Physically, that's pretty demanding. Mentally, even more so. The best way to handle that pressure is to do as much of the thinking in advance

---

8   This remarkable outfit is known as 'sub fusc'. The carnation is a different colour depending on which exam is being taken. Oxford will burn to the ground before the university drops sub fusc – because the students repeatedly insist on keeping it.

as possible, and let the essay crisis muscle memory do the rest.

The second quality, then, is planning and tactics. Turning over a final exam paper is a bone-chilling moment for students doing any course. Most fear that they will find a set of questions they have no idea how to answer. With PPE, the situation is a little different. Every candidate turning over the paper does so in the expectation that they won't have the faintest idea how to answer at least half the questions. That's OK – they've planned for that. The worry is all down to whether their revision gamble has paid off. They will have spent the past few months trying to remember – or often learning for the first time – material they haven't seen since the first term of second year.

By Christmas of your third year, the compulsory parts of the PPE course are essentially finished. There are no more tutorials to attend, no more essays to write. It is for you, and you alone, to determine what to get up to in the six months between now and your first exam. As far as the university is concerned, this could be spent further refining your crisp-eating habits. Nobody is checking.

One strategy for success in PPE exams is to spend that six months learning all the possible material that could come up in a paper, thereby giving you a fair chance of answering any question. Given the sprawling scope of most of the papers, that's an unfeasibly large amount of work for virtually anyone.

This is where the tactics come in. The real question for a PPE finalist now becomes: how much do I need to know? For a paper where you have to answer three questions, the obvious choice is to pick three topics to cram. Unfortunately, Oxford's examiners are wise to this, and are not above combining two topics into a single question, or omitting some altogether. This points to a strategy of preparing four, five or six topics for each exam, depending on how bold you're feeling. The moment you turn over the paper is the moment your choices prove right – or disastrously wrong.

Let's say the tactics have paid off. There are at least three questions on the paper that include nods to topics you recognise with confidence. What are the examiners really looking for in those essays?

Unusually for Oxford, the mark scheme for PPE is

both clear and publicly available, so there's no point reproducing it here. Even so, it's worth giving a sense of what they really mean.

If you got a third-class degree, you probably turned up to the exam room with a bad poker hand, having done very little work or planning. The cards did not fall in your favour. PPE thirds are rare, with no more than two or three awarded in each year. With the exception of a few unlucky people who suffered a genuine distraction from studies, most people with a third in PPE have chosen to get one. This is usually by virtue of being wholly absorbed by some other part of student life, like comedy, politics or playing pinball and watching *Neighbours*. Thirds are for people who found something better to do than studying, and quite often they turn out to have made the right decision. Because Oxford is, in the final analysis, British to a fault, deep respect is given to the glorious failure that a third represents. It is not called a gentleman's third for nothing.

This kind of respect is not accorded to a lower-second-class degree (or II.2 in Oxford parlance). People with II.2s have committed a cardinal sin in the eyes of intellectual snobs – they made an effort and it didn't pay off. Lower-second degrees often find themselves the victims of a revision gamble gone awry; they either end up reading too little or too much. Too little, and there is nothing to go on the bones of a decent argument; too much, and their argument becomes hidden from view entirely.

For an upper second – awarded to about three-quarters of the PPE intake – you've read just the right amount, nicely balanced the two sides of the argument, and left it at that. This is where the revision gamble has paid off perfectly; most of the exam itself could be completed on autopilot, because the essay answers were pretty much written before the candidate had even sat down.

For a first, there are two paths. The more romantic path is much like the third-class degree, except the gods smile on you. These candidates turn up with not much more than a pen and a smile, and walk out with the prize. As well as having some serious swag, this strategy takes incredible luck or genuine genius. It's also very rare. There's a popular idea that Oxford is full of god-tier blaggers who try rolling the dice like this; foppish men and women who briefly put down their Chartreuse and crumpled packet of cigarettes in the punt before sloughing over to Exam Schools to bang out reams of sumptuously argued prose.

The truth is that there is maybe one person – at most – in the entire year with the genius and self-belief to pull this romantic ideal off. It only seems more common because (a) people tend to remember the one bastard brilliant enough to do this, (b) this is the type of person who tends to feature prominently in public life later on, and (c) other people who actually tried rather hard to get their first prefer to pretend they were that bastard because it offers a much better anecdote.

For mere mortals, there is an alternative and less glamorous path to a first-class degree – work very hard, have a clear plan, and get to the point where you're confident enough to play your tutorial game against the published texts. If you've read enough to angrily argue against the ideas your examiners expect you to know, and you can give that criticism sufficient force to suggest you really have read them, then you're in good shape to scrape the extra four or five marks that let you spend the next fifty years airily referring to your first-class degree.

And there you have it. You now know everything you need to be a successful PPE student.

PPE is the perfect preparation for bluffers in public life. It is the degree where one is presented as knowing everything, and it provides a bluffer with the tools to confidently give that impression. Beneath the surface, it teaches you exactly how to do just enough, in just enough time, to make sure the mask doesn't easily slip off.

Of course, that's not the whole story. There are a few other qualities that help. PPE is a course laden with bias, both conscious and unconscious. Certain people thrive while others flounder. That's true of pretty much any academic pursuit you can think of; arguably the whole point of examinations is to reward a particular combination of skill and personality. However, if you accept the idea that PPE is a path into the elite, the biases become a lot more worthy of scrutiny.

The adversarial set-up of PPE's teaching methods is a format that rewards a mild form of dramatic performance. That doesn't necessarily mean you have to be an extrovert or outright confrontational to succeed, but it's a lot less painful if you're the kind of person who draws energy out of the sheer joy of arguing. It's possible to start your PPE degree without this confidence already baked into your soul – typically, state school entrants start behind their privately educated peers – but few leave without it.

Even better, if you can see arguing as a game, and shake hands with no hard feelings at the end (even when your own position and reputation have been publicly ripped apart, leaving you feeling like your brain has spent an hour in a threshing machine), then PPE will work for you. Not being too ideological helps, too. Caring deeply about the topic at hand will only serve to distract you from the game.

Some of the biases in PPE are more subtle. It is not immediately obvious that PPE is a male-dominated environment, yet it is from admission to graduation. Between 2015 and 2017, Oxford received 2,462 applications for PPE. Sixty-seven per cent of those came from men, who ended up getting 65 per cent of the places.

As we've explained, PPE is ultimately an exam-driven course. Studies have repeatedly shown that courses that heavily rely on exams (rather than coursework) tend to favour boys.

The content of PPE also tends to assume a certain frame of reference. If your background is from a western European, liberal democratic tradition, you'll feel right at home. Other world views get much less of a look-in. In fairness to the university, there are several options papers that offer mind-broadening insights on different ideologies or political systems. But it's perfectly possible to sail through the whole course without touching the sides of anything that doesn't comply with the default setting of a medium-sized European nation state. Many do just that.

So, provided you're a highly confident, westernised, cheerfully argumentative and usually male student who has read our thirty-minute guide, PPE should be no problem for you.

Just imagine a country run by people like that.

# Part II

# Part II

# Bluffing up

**E**DUCATION PREPARES US for adult life. For some of us, it gives us knowledge and insights we go on to apply in work. Medicine, engineering, accountancy, law, mechanics; qualifications are a hurdle for those wanting to enter a profession. Any discipline that needs some kind of deep expertise is not a friendly place for those predisposed to spreading themselves thinly across many subjects.

Yet, for a country that remains incredibly snobbish about vocational education versus going to a university, there is an irony that PPE, perhaps its most notorious degree, is actually the ultimate vocational course. The subject knowledge that graduates come away with is neither here nor there. It's the skills and attitude it leaves behind that are the real learning – and for many who take it, the subject matter is of less academic interest than the course's status as a route into politics, the civil service or the City.

Even so, for those schooled in bluffing, the career choice is less obvious. One could renounce one's commitment to generalism and retrain in something specific, or go all in. If the latter, where's a smart bluffer to go?

Every career has some form of discrimination and barrier to entry; be that intellectual ability, a certain professional qualification, physical attractiveness, a particular attitude or something more sinister. The trick for bluffers looking to build their career is to find places where the barriers work in their favour. Which industries favour intellectual firepower over high-level formal qualifications, skilled improvisation over thoughtful introspection, argument and strategy over elbow grease and delivery?

Fortunately, several industries are built on exactly these qualities, and they happen to be those that profoundly shape the country. Politics, government, consultancy, media and all their associated hangers-on are largely driven, influenced and led by bluffers. This wasn't always the case, or at least not to this extent. In times of crisis, experts used to be a somewhat more common and visible feature at the top of British journalism, officialdom and politics. So how are the career generalists getting in, and how did they end up taking over?

\*   \*   \*

Not every bluffer is power-hungry, money-grabbing or status-driven. Just because someone is biased towards generalism doesn't mean they will reach the top. We'll focus here on the ones who do, mostly because it's the behaviour of the most successful bluffers that has the biggest impact on everyone else.

The key trait in common for areas where generalists and bluffers thrive is a focus on quick mastery of new material, and reacting quickly and confidently to events. This manifests itself most obviously on Twitter, where named commentators and popular anonymous users alike will appear to shift in expertise hour by hour. One moment, the account is an expert on the use and history of Russian nerve agents. The next, it's an expert in analysing the complex politics of the Syria conflict. Days later, it's setting forth in apparently great depth about competition law, welfare policy or tackling tax dodging – all with equal confidence.

That trend is unnerving when you watch it unfold on social media, but all the more worrying when you begin to see how it plays out in public life: the ministers, civil servants and journalists who get ahead are the ones who can have a successful 'essay crisis' – finding out just enough about a huge and complex topic within the space of hours to write the story to nail the crisis, or the memo to avert it, or to survive the House of Commons debate where someone tries to make it fatal.

We might hope for government and the media to be focused on the long term, to be trying to explain what the ramifications of political decisions will be in years and decades to come, what the risks are, and what we need to weigh up. At their best, that's what these systems do – but in practice, most of the time, most of these organisations aren't looking much further ahead than the next few weeks.

In journalism, a sharp and decisive news story on the

current crisis will make a far sexier front page than a measured, considered piece taking in the long view and folding in the nuance. For ministers, the questions at hand are usually related to working out how to manage a current crisis or put through a bit of policy that's landed on their desk. And for those in the civil service, the best way to rise is to look at getting through whatever policy has the minister's eye. Simply managing and running programmes agreed years ago are vital roles, but not good for the ambitious.

Former chair of the parole board Nick Hardwick – who himself stepped down amid the political row over the decision to grant parole to convicted rapist John Worboys – shared advice summarising much of political and civil service culture, and the traits they value. Quoting 'one of the civil servants [he] learned the most from', he wrote of the Home Office: 'The people who get on here are those that can write a good minute which gets a minister out of trouble. Not those who can run things so they don't get into trouble in the first place.'

Such workplaces are rife for bluffers: the skills they have, either naturally or taught through PPE or similar courses, are well suited. They have many subtle tricks in their arsenal to get noticed in workplaces which still often rely on patronage – coming to the attention of senior ministers or editors is a common way to fast-track a bluffer's early and mid-career.

These tactics include knowing how and when to speak in meetings; an extension of skills learned in private school or Oxbridge tutorials. Speaking early is wise in a meeting where you don't know much – the relatively obvious points are still available to be made, and you can frame the conversation before quietly sitting back. By contrast, if you've got a killer detail or argument you think others lack – especially if it could prove decisive – wait until the end, so it sticks with people. This and dozens of other tricks – speaking in the intakes of breath that others leave, knowing when to drop a rhetorical question, knowing just how much research to do – are used (including by us) to get attention.

It often works – it's how leader conferences (where newspapers pick their editorial line) work – but it's worth looking at how it operates in each of the different spheres this book focuses on.

# Ministers and MPs

Of all the fields that come to be dominated by bluffers, politics perhaps has the best excuses: so much of what's expected at the top of the profession is about doing well at local and national gatherings, speaking on TV and radio, and holding forth in the House of Commons, whether from the despatch box or the back benches. As such, politicians can hardly be criticised for possessing good public speaking skills – it is, after all, a big part of the job.

But that doesn't mean there's not a problem with expertise in politics – as signalled by complaints of the rise of the 'professional politician', a trait which seems tied to the long-term plummeting trust in the profession: according to pollster Ipsos MORI, only around 17 per cent of people trust politicians in general to tell the truth, with just 19 per cent trusting Cabinet ministers.

A rival pollster, YouGov, looked into the reasons for this mistrust in a separate piece of research, asking members of the public which traits they thought were unsuitable in leading politicians. It turns out that the personal traits usually associated with a tabloid frenzy and subsequent resignation statement aren't what bother the public most. Only 13 per cent would rule out a politician who had taken Class A drugs when younger, while only 15 per cent would rule out someone who had been a member of a hard-right party (10 per cent would rule out a former communist). Just 14 per cent of respondents said an MP who had run as a married heterosexual who later admitted they were gay was unsuitable for office, and only 9 per cent would rule out someone who had been bankrupt.

While we've generally got more forgiving and tolerant of politicians' personal crises, there are two traits the public remain much less happy about. Yet it is these which are much more common. Thirty-eight per cent of the poll's respondents said they thought a politician who had been 'to Eton and [didn't] understand how normal people live' couldn't be trusted. Fifty-five per cent said someone was unsuitable for office if they had never had a 'real' job outside of politics, think tanks or journalism.

In other words, the public are apparently more sick of bluffers in public life than drug users or philanderers. We're more accepting of MPs having had a youthful dabbling in fascism than we are of people with skills and abilities honed to navigate the political sphere but not much outside it. People doubtless want politicians and their teams to have these skills, but they expect more from outside it, and increasingly they're not seeing it in their politics. How much of this attitude runs more than skin-deep is hard to say. Jeremy Corbyn is one of the country's most trusted politicians at the time of writing, yet he has been a professional politician for more than three decades. Ironically, Jeremy's accidental masterstroke has been pulling off the trick of not looking or behaving like a professional hack.

To call politicians (or at least some of them) bluffers isn't intended to doubt their dedication to public service, or that they work hard. Many are exceptionally conscientious. The life of a backbench MP is an unglamorous one – they constantly need to shore up support in their constituencies with a relentless series of local events, canvassing and fairs; as austerity bites and MPs pick up the slack, they have a huge caseload of constituency work; and the ones who want to get things done in Parliament need to put the hours in at the House, too.

The road to Parliament, though, especially through professional politics, is one well suited to a clever bluffer. One of the lowest rungs on the political ladder is working for an MP, jobs with lousy pay and terrible hours. There are two roles: constituency caseworkers, who deal with welfare and other issues raised by constituents, and parliamentary researchers. Those hoping to climb the ladder fast will aim for the latter: not only is the role based in Westminster, giving a better chance to rub shoulders and move up, but it involves working on the projects your MP is keen to advance on the biggest political stage – whether preparing them for debates, drafting written questions or campaigning.

The people who do well at that will advance, either moving to work for more prominent MPs or shifting to become a special advisor (or its equivalent in opposition), often with the aim of moving from there to become an MP or an advisor to a senior minister.

Other moves in the ecosystem that can still build towards the parliamentary route include jumping across to become a newspaper columnist – of which more later – or joining a think tank. These institutions ostensibly exist to help formulate policies and gather evidence beyond what parties can officially endorse, but they face their own pressures. The organisations have funders to attract, and want to seek coverage. A think tank that is happy to jump up quickly with bold policies with just enough back-up will often prove more successful than a more thorough but less daring one.

By these routes, or through local politics, or through trade unions, a bright candidate could suddenly find themselves up for selection to become an MP, and if they can convince a few dozen local party members that they're the best fit for the job, they're in Parliament. And, as has been noted since the days of *Yes Minister*, if they can acquit themselves with a reasonable amount of competence on the back bench, build up one or two of the right allies and get a little decent PR, it's quite a small jump to become a minister or shadow minister.

There are around 45 million people eligible to become an MP, and only 650 of them at any given time can make it there, meaning there are in theory at least 2.1 million potential candidates for each seat. But by the time they've passed that hurdle, becoming a minister is a much lower bar. At the time of writing, the government has 109 paid ministers, with a further nine unpaid. Most of those – except those who come from the Lords – get picked from a pool of just 316 Conservative MPs. One in three is pretty good odds.

The job of a minister – or that of an opposing shadow minister – lies in learning a brief you may have had zero knowledge of or influence over, and finding a way to either attack or defend the government record on it. Often the minister in charge of implementing a decision (or defending a mistake) will have had no say in making it – and might even in private have disagreed with it – making it little surprise the role is suited to bluffers.

Tom Hamilton, a former advisor to Ed Miliband in his role as opposition leader, and co-author of *Punch & Judy Politics*, a history of Prime Minister's Questions, says that most ministers do grasp some level of detail – very few totally wing it – but mastering things quickly is essential to the job.

'It's about understanding the brief, at least up to a certain level of expertise which falls short of real expert knowledge but goes beyond reading a few news reports,' he explains. 'In government, ministers and the PM will have quite detailed briefing and lines to take, and will generally have discussed this with relevant officials and advisors, because they need to think about what the hardest questions are and what answers they want to give.'

Hamilton notes that little attention is generally given to MPs' background or interests when considering ministerial appointments, to the point where expertise can be detrimental. 'There are a few people with a strong interest or expertise who get particular jobs, but that's usually at the junior ministerial or shadow ministerial level,' he says, before explaining the bizarre logic that works against promoting specialists. '[Knowledge] can be career-limiting, because you're still probably not going to get promoted to the Cabinet/shadow Cabinet, and moving you sideways, which would help you develop your career, is obviously silly because you're in the job you're in for your specific expertise.'

Instead, Hamilton supports the conclusion that the modern view of experts has hardly moved on from the Churchillian adage of 'on tap, not on top'. They're there to be leaned upon for support where they back up what you already think; to be cited in the chamber, where they can't be challenged.

'Politicians often recognise that they're not experts, and look for experts to hide behind – but they're quite bad at evaluating expertise, because they're mostly looking to use it to back up their positions,' he concludes.

> You know, the 'We should introduce a land value tax – and that's not just me saying it, it's Professor Joe Bloggs of Oxford University' style of argument. Everyone is always looking for third-party independent endorsement, and that helps to incentivise the creation of bodies that can provide it or appear to provide it.

There is one final corner in which experts can reside in politics, and that's the House of Lords: expert scientists, doctors, academics and others are often appointed to the upper chamber without political affiliation, in theory leaving them able to shape debate and legislation with the benefit of their expertise. The reality leaves a little more to be desired. The group of crossbench peers makes up just 181 out of 799 peers eligible to vote, fewer than either the Conservative or Labour contingents, and on their own are only able to influence or persuade others, rather than shift the law directly.

This impotence is heightened by just how toothless the House of Lords can be: they are ultimately unable to block any legislation that's in a party's manifesto, and can only delay legislation by one year in the case of a proper showdown. They're also unable to vote on money bills – anything deciding where and how public money gets spent – and Prime Ministers have additionally shown themselves willing and able to pack the chamber with new peers to shift the balance in their favour. One of the small nooks in political life better set up to house experts is almost designed to make sure their voice can't be heard. Still – at least politicians have the expertise of the professional civil service to lean on.

## Whitehall and public services

Of all Britain's national institutions, the civil service comes in for the least scrutiny. At first glance, this seems strange. There are far more people employed in the bureaucracy than in journalism or politics,[9] and the inner workings of government touch everyone's lives now and again. Whitehall and its many tendrils slip under the radar because officials operate in a world that is highly complex, devoted to detail, and deeply dull. This is not an accident. As attention spans grow shorter, Whitehall skilfully uses boredom like an invisibility cloak. Few sweep it away to find the gasping two-stroke engine hiding beneath the bonnet of a bureaucratic machine puttering along in much the same way it has done for 150 years. The civil service is often described as a Rolls-Royce. This is true – it usually behaves exactly as you'd expect a 150-year-old car to behave.

The other obvious reason senior civil servants hove into view less frequently than their political or media brethren is because the top layer of officialdom actively avoids the limelight. If you were shown the names and photos of the three dozen or so people currently running the country's great offices of state, the chances are

---

9   There are about 400,000 civil servants working in the UK, compared to about 70,000 journalists and fewer still in politics.

you wouldn't recognise a single one. Who are these shadowy figures?

You might expect public service to be a world relatively free of generalists. The complexity of government and the specialised knowledge it demands would suggest this is no place for a bluffer. For the most part, this is true. But at the top, the very shape of the civil service has made it one of the most notable bluffer-led institutions. Bluffers are more deeply ground into the fabric of Whitehall than anywhere else in national life. To understand why, you need to go back to its Victorian roots.

When the modern civil service took shape in the 1850s, it did so in response to accusations that the bureaucracy was a 'sick service', stuffed full of malingerers and kept running by a small handful of energetic men who were collapsing under the strain of keeping the show on the road. One of those energetic men, Sir Charles Trevelyan, told a parliamentary committee how he got up early, spent three hours before breakfast reading his papers, then worked at the Treasury until late in the evening, returning home too exhausted for anything except sleep. Stress had already carried off three of his predecessors as head of the Treasury. The solution, he argued, was to create a meritocratic organisation, setting tough exams that kept out the dead wood, and making sure those people who passed the tests were easily interchangeable with one another. His boss, the then Chancellor William Gladstone, took him at his word.

Trevelyan's plans – which still amount to the most recent revolutionary change to British official life – sought to create 'a non-political administrative class educated in the moral values of a liberal education further developed by a reformed Oxford and Cambridge'. It also created classes of civil servants. At the top, the First Division, would be the small handful of successful exam-passers who could turn their hand to any of the 3,000 or so senior posts in government.[10] All the rest – the technical, clerical and mechanical skills that made up the vast majority of public officialdom (and still do) – were kept separate from the First Division tribe, subject to different rules, skills and behaviours.

So far, so Victorian. In the intervening century and a

---

10  The union for senior civil servants is still called the First Division Association.

half, Whitehall's Upstairs, Downstairs approach has not stood completely still. The senior civil service employs women now, for example. The number of Permanent Secretaries[11] declaring their membership of a Pall Mall club has fallen precipitously. In recent decades, and by their own account, the most called-upon source of counsel for senior officials has become broadsheet newspapers, as opposed to former university tutors. Even so, the basic design of Britain's permanent civil service has stayed almost exactly the same. So has its expectations of the leadership.

The day-to-day job of a senior civil servant is in many ways similar to that of any executive: sitting in meetings all day, giving the impression that you know what you're talking about. There are two things that make it unusual.

The first is Whitehall's attitude to leadership. Business books pontificate at length about the difference between good 'managers', who get stuff done and look after their people, and good 'leaders', who set direction and are full

---

11 Permanent Secretaries are the most senior grade of official. Sir Humphrey Appleby, the serpentine antihero of *Yes Minister*, was a Permanent Secretary.

of visionary inspiration. But when the chips are down, the senior civil servant's job is neither of these. The clue is in the name – they are there to serve their ministers. By design, the top of the civil service has always been home to many people who are superb servants, but many of them can't lead or manage their way out of a paper bag. This leads to risibly underqualified people being put in charge of some of the country's biggest and most complicated organisations.

Being skilled at handling ministers – a core bluffer competency – is what allows official careers to flourish against a background of repeated leadership disaster. Over the course of eight years, Dame Lin Homer managed to be rapped for presiding over a vote-rigging scandal in Birmingham City Council; lead the UK Border Agency over the period when the organisation was described as a 'Whitehall farce' and Windrush records were destroyed; lead the Department of Transport when it wasted £100 million on mishandling the West Coast rail franchise letting process; and lead HMRC while it gave an 'unambitious and woefully inadequate' response to customer service woes. Yet Homer was described as 'a highly effective chief executive and the right person to lead HMRC' by her minister, David Gauke.

The second quirk of senior officialdom is the set-piece events: select committee appearances, ministerial meetings and writing submissions. The first we've already talked about. The only real difference between a minister's and an official's appearance in front of a committee is that the former should do their best to convey authority and leadership, whereas the latter should strive to avoid saying anything of value.

Ministerial meetings take place in private, in the higher floors of departmental buildings in and around Whitehall. In these, the objective of a senior civil servant is ultimately to persuade the minister that she knows what she is talking about, and that the course of action she is proposing is the right one. Ministerial meetings are rarely one-to-one affairs; a small phalanx of officials will typically appear. Some will be there to take notes, others will be fighting to ensure their bit of departmental turf gets a fair hearing. In many respects, this is exactly like a PPE tutorial, and those who thrive in the format tend to have spent their formative years deploying the tactics we described in Part I.

University echoes through the other set-piece of official life: the ministerial submission. A submission is a paper provided to a minister on a topic where he or she needs to make a decision. In most cases, officials will present their political boss with a few options and then recommend one of them. Submissions are the professionalisation of essay crises, and work in much the same way. Thrown together at speed, they are written and formatted to make it appear as if the author has fully grasped the issue, encompassing the myriad of choices a minister might make. Lengthy annexes are appended to give further credence to this impression. Ministers, who are busy, will tend to agree rather than argue – especially if they trust the official who sent up the paper.

Building close relationships with colleagues as you simultaneously try to haul yourself above them, like crabs trapped in a bucket, is how a senior civil servant's career echoes the civilities of tutorial life. Become good at this while pleasing a succession of ministers, and the keys to a long and successful official career are yours.

The bluffers who make good in the senior civil service are of a different character to those in politics or the media. Relatively few of them threw their weight around in student newspapers or joined elite Oxbridge vomiting societies. They are usually quieter, industrious, conscientious types. Blaggers can be busy too. Yet because of their generalist nature, all the frenzied activity at the top of government usually generates more heat than light. The lack of delivery is no accident. Delivery makes you stand out. Most civil servants don't like standing out.

By personality, senior civil servants tend to be less visibly egomaniacal than their bluffing peers. But the ego is still there; it is just that for a top official it takes on a different shape to that of a politician. By preference and institutional design, very few senior civil servants are ever completely responsible for the work they are doing. This makes this clan of bluffers much less covetous of individual achievement. As a quid pro quo, they are much more skittish about being held accountable. The buck doesn't stop in the civil service; it gets shared around until everyone has a small enough piece.

One of the civil service's achievements is sustaining itself in pretty much the same form for such a long time. It does this by skilfully hiring in its own image. The civil service fast stream is a popular choice for university graduates. It's competitive: over 20,000 apply each year for a thousand places. Like the rest of the civil service, strides have been made to improve the visible diversity of the scheme: in 2015, the gender split was roughly 50/50, and nearly 10 per cent of appointees were disabled. Diversity of experience was less in evidence. A fifth of successful applicants went to Oxbridge; less than 5 per cent of recruits had parents who worked in manual jobs. Eighty per cent of the new intake came from parents who made their career in the professions.

Fast-streamers are hired as the next generation to occupy the First Division. Their apprenticeship – a three-year programme – is designed to sheep-dip them in the experience of being a senior civil servant. It does this very well, though perhaps not in the way it is officially intended. In theory, being a fast-streamer earns you a greater training budget, more management support and some career-planning expertise. In practice, the real benefits involve getting used to what you've signed up for three decades of: being paid less than one's private sector peers, enduring crap management, working very long hours, being shunted from department to department with limited personal choice and even less notice, and being part of a Cabinet Office-run scheme that is shambolically administered.

Despite taking well over a year to secure their place, a third of fast-streamers leave their job before the end of the scheme. Those who stay have developed the tenacity and support to deal with the bullshit. In the near-universal view of those who go through it, the most valuable part of the whole experience is the relationships fast-streamers build with their peer group, many of whom they will keep in touch with throughout their career in government. Building a tight network and the ability to cheerfully handle abject organisational dysfunction – these are the true qualities expected in the future leaders of our civil service. Deep subject knowledge is of no value at all.

In recent decades, the civil service has found it harder to recruit enough proto-bluffers to mould into tomorrow's mandarins; whereas once a job in government offered a golden ticket, today's bluffers have more lucrative and appealing options. This is especially true in local government, which successive national governments have stripped of funding and relevance. To fill this gap, governments have instead gone down the route of hiring bluffers off the peg.

One form is the drive-by executive, an interim boss who swoops in for a year or so to shout at people in a fairly haphazard fashion before collecting a large cheque. Several people have made a lucrative late-stage career out of this, hopping between councils and NHS Trusts that have an inexhaustible demand for leadership with a 'track record', even if – like Lin Homer – that record includes failure on a national scale. At the most extreme end of the scale, such interim managers can be paid at rates far in excess of even the most senior permanent managers: an NHS Trust in Enfield paid a 'director of recovery' £34,000 a month for five months, while another paid over £90,000 for a three-month 'turnaround director'.

An equally common trope is the rise of management

consultants. Like the civil service, management consultancy is one of those rare well-paid disciplines that doesn't demand any formal professional qualifications. It is also big business. Central government in the UK spends more than £4 billion on consultancy; the NHS and local government billions more. In the wake of Brexit, literally thousands of consultants are streaming into Whitehall.

Drive-by executives and management consultants have the same appeal to officialdom: they are pre-vetted as being sound, dependable blaggers. This confidence acts as a form of intellectual freemasonry. Even if their appointment ultimately proves disastrous – and it often does – the people who hired them can't be blamed for that. No one ever gets fired for hiring McKinsey or IBM.

Occasionally, ministers have tried to use Whitehall's instinctive trust in sound blaggers to create political advantages for themselves, surrounding themselves with hordes of special advisors who already speak their language and who offer some protection from officials' own blagging dialect. This is usually counterproductive; the civil service is wise to others using their trick. The

First Division tolerates a few politically appointed blaggers, on the grounds that they do jobs that senior civil servants don't want to do. When ministers try to make appointments outside those tight boundaries, Whitehall does not hesitate to call foul. The ultra example of this kind of backlash lies with the attempted appointment of serial blagger – and friend to several Cabinet ministers – Toby Young to the new watchdog, the Office for Students. Young was appointed over many seemingly more qualified candidates in a process which was later heavily criticised by a civil service commission investigation. Young had already lost the role after a series of offensive tweets were resurfaced, and a journalistic investigation revealed his apparent support for eugenics.[12] 'The decision on whether or not to appoint one candidate in particular was heavily influenced,' the report into the hiring archly noted, 'not by [the interview] panel, but by special advisers, notably from 10 Downing Street.' To be welcomed – or at least tolerated

---

12 We did not expect the topic of eugenics to arise once, let alone twice, when we set out researching this book.

– behind the curtain by officialdom, you have to be willing to stay at least fairly quiet.

The face of officialdom may have changed over the past 150 years, but the generalist brains behind it really haven't. While politicians are in charge of determining the direction of the country, senior civil servants are responsible for working out how to get there. Perhaps it's little wonder we often get lost along the way. Well, at least we have Britain's famously vigorous free press to help us pick through the bones of our problems.

## The media

In the rankings of public trust, journalists rank just ahead of politicians, and just behind estate agents. This doesn't look good for anyone concerned.

The media is a slightly different beast from the previous two categories discussed in that it doesn't directly make or implement laws – but, by being the route through which the public finds out about the activities of the first two groups, it carries a disproportionate impact on them. If the UK's journalists as a pack have decided to focus on one particular issue, you can be sure that's where ministers' and civil servants' focus is forced to be.

That means that what journalists choose to focus on – and what makes it onto the bulletins and front pages – becomes of great importance, and there's not too many people who would look at the papers each day and feel entirely happy about exactly what's chosen.

At this particular moment, the media is in the middle of a huge wave of change: many newsrooms have made serious cuts in the numbers of their experienced staff, often letting specialists and experienced reporters go as readers shift to online. The entire industry is contending with plummeting ad revenues and falling print sales. This has meant many newsrooms are now filled with aspiring young writers in their early twenties with workloads which make any kind of specialism or investigation impossible.

Writers in one national newsroom speak of being required to produce a story every forty-five minutes. That isn't forty-five minutes to write a story – it's forty-five minutes to research the story, write it, select the pictures and come up with a headline and other online 'furniture'. A workload of eight to ten stories at a time is typical. But while this contributes to the shallowness of today's media coverage, and will certainly crowd out the ability of new writers to become specialists in the future, it's doesn't explain why bluffing is already so deeply ingrained. For that, you need to look at what kind of journalist becomes senior enough to routinely write front-page news. It won't come as a surprise: it's the bluffers[13] who prosper.

The most obvious target for this charge is the political lobby – the closed-door club of journalists tasked with covering politics with an archaic and (to the public, at least) incomprehensible set of rules that began to look outdated roughly a century ago. The principle of the system is largely designed to protect ministers and their spokespeople from ever having to deal directly with people who know policy detail – so if health news is dominating the headlines, for example, the health correspondent won't be the one to speak with the minister

---

13 If it has come as a surprise, we can really only suggest you jump back a bit and read some of the book over again.

concerned. Instead, it will be a reporter specialising in politics.

Criticism of the lobby shouldn't be confused with suggesting that the journalists concerned are lazy or stupid. Lobby journalists work some of the most gruelling hours in the profession, and it's not a place where anyone stupid could prosper for long. Some of the most talented people are part of the lobby. This is a bit of a shame.

The lobby system is designed to help make sure politicians speak to people who are familiar with the rules of the game: lobby journalists receive advance text on speeches and they get two briefings in a day, a formal one in the morning and a more informal one afterwards. They 'huddle' after big events like Prime Minister's Questions, annual Budget speeches or similar, where they are briefed with extra details after the public debates.

A particular feature of the system is the tacit understanding of intricate rules around what is on and off the record, with numerous layers in between the two. In the UK lobby system, spokespeople are never named, meaning the morning briefings always appear from 'a spokesman' or 'the spokesman' for the Prime Minister. It remains deeply questionable whether such shorthand makes any sense to the average reader, especially when there are a lot of other artful attributions that signify unauthorised briefing, whether that's 'friends of [Cabinet minister]',[14] a 'senior minister',[15] or a 'well-respected backbencher'.[16]

The world of the lobby is small: it is a limited number of journalists interacting with a small pool of ministers and their shadows, and the pool of advisors who surround them – a group of people with all of the bluffing skills we have listed. Bluffing almost becomes a specialism in itself. On both sides, everyone becomes good at playing the game, picking each word carefully so as to create or decode the half-truths that avert or uncover scandals.

Lobby journalists even work separately from their colleagues, rarely turning up to their newsrooms. They

---

14  'The Cabinet minister themselves, or their spokesperson'.
15  'Someone not in the Cabinet who always helps me out'.
16  'Someone who'll always give me a quote, even when I can't get a minister to talk'.

socialise with one another and with politicians, set apart
from the rest of their own industry and equally far from
the people affected by the policies they're writing about.
This means the focus of the story is often on what matters to the sources concerned – what does the passage or
otherwise of a bill mean for internal Cabinet politics?
Where does the blame lie for a policy being shelved?
What does the last week in politics mean for the run-
ners and riders for next party leader?

The political lobby's stranglehold over access to official
information and announcements – especially the background briefings around them – means that on big policy
news days, the lobby are in the driving seat. A government bill might run to hundreds of pages, and reams of
technical detail that a specialist might know the ins and
outs of, but the front-page news story (or the top slot on
broadcast) will likely sit with the lobby hack. That pushes
the bluffer's version of the news – often the nice grabby
announcement either the government or the opposition
party wants – onto the front pages. The specialist reporter,
if the outlet still has one, will see their story relegated to an
analysis slot, often many pages deep into the newspaper.

The lobby is just one symptom of journalism's uneasy relationship with specialism. The longer a journalist stays on a particular beat – assuming the paper has kept specialists, as many have removed these expensive reporters in favour of younger, cheaper generalists – the more likely editors are to worry that they've been 'captured' by their beat. A new reporter might see a jump in crime statistics and offer it up as a juicy lead story. An experienced specialist may try to say the same jump in figures isn't a real news story, as it's just (for example) the result of a change in how the statistics are collated. In this instance, the generalist is offering up an apparently good story to the news desk, while the specialist is offering up nothing. It's not hard to see which a news desk might prefer.

The epidemiologist and science writer Ben Goldacre has been noting this phenomenon in science writing for more than a decade. In multiple cases he has flagged, a paper's science or health reporter will reject a press release with a nonsense story – such as 'Blue Monday', a PR-confected story with a bogus statistical formula for the most depressing day of the year – only for the news desk to instead ask a non-specialist reporter to write it up anyway, because it will get lots of online clicks.

In the news section, bluffers are constrained, at least somewhat, by the conventions of reporting – keeping opinion to a minimum and at least trying to reflect the views of all sides involved. When things move to the opinion section, things get ugly. Predicting the future is not an easy job for any commentator, but many opinion writers' barefaced ability to perform rapid U-turns is rivalled only by the most expensive of supercars.

The same writer will shamelessly and rapidly write one week about why the current government is stable and talented and the sun shines from the Prime Minister's nethers. Two weeks of setbacks later, and they'll write and explain why any fool could have seen this coming, and how the Prime Minister could have easily prevented it. If you would ever like to have an event explained by someone who utterly failed to see it coming, look no further than UK opinion pages, whose hindsight is second to none.

Finally, there's the leader column: the editorials that serve as the newspaper's 'official' opinion on the events of the previous day. News reporters – whether specialists or from the lobby – get nowhere near deciding on these, or even weighing in at the meeting. Outside experts are not required. If the paper and its leader writer are feeling especially diligent, they may read the news copy running in their own paper – but that will often be the limit of their research. These columns that spell out the official stance of news institutions often more than a century old are generally pulled together by bright recent grads – with one or two older hands making sure they don't do anything that will accidentally irritate the owner – after swift morning meetings. These rising stars then often go on to leading roles in the comment pages, or straight into high political office. Plenty of Cabinet ministers, including Michael Gove, had their start in leader writing. It is perhaps the ultimate bluffer's incubator.

❧    ❧    ❧

The three institutions we've set out each have their own reasons to prize generalists, and to become dominated by them. Each of those on its own comes to show some negative consequences for the functioning of public life, but there's a broader effect when all three interact. None of these institutions acts in isolation: the short-termism and generalism of the media builds pressure on ministers to respond in kind, who in turn put pressure on the civil service to act. If the civil service falls into line with such pressure to create or amend policy to suit headlines then such laws could fall apart, generating new headlines – creating a never-ending cycle. Next, we're going to look at what the real-world consequences of that cycle are, for all of us.

# Part III

# Living under bluffocracy

B RITAIN ISN'T SHORT on problems at present. The country is in the midst of a productivity crisis, a housing deficit, the long-term effects of austerity, and of course the small matter of Brexit and its aftermath. Against that backdrop, why bother with the employment culture of the establishment? If this is how it has always been, what's the point of worrying about it now?

The bluffocracy may be a less obvious problem, but in many ways it is a more serious, insidious one than what's currently sitting on top of the country's in-tray. Hardwired blagging is woven into the cause of many challenges we're facing, shaping the short-termism and lack of detail that plagues our national institutions, and contributing to the crisis of trust in British public life.

We're left with the options of continuing to keep putting out whatever dumpster fire looms large today, in a game of legislative whack-a-mole, or tackling the underlying cause. Here, we try to set out why bluffing culture contributes to some of the country's deeper problems – and suggest a few things we could begin to do to tackle it.

\*　\*　\*

The effect of loading up Britain's boardrooms and Cabinet table with generalist bluffers is not always subtle or indirect. The skills and values that our institutions prize can have a big role in shaping their most obvious public failures. One such case is the scandal around government attempts to deport people who arrived legally to the UK in the 1950s and '60s – the so-called Windrush generation – as a result of the government's 'hostile environment' policy.

The scandal unfolded almost as an archetype of how Home Office controversies unfold. The deportations of people legally in the country happened as a foreseeable result of a deliberate policy to challenge people as they rent property or access public services, which was introduced by Theresa May when she was Home Secretary. The government had received multiple warnings through the media – if not leading front pages – and private consultations with MPs and others, which had gone largely ignored until it became a much bigger story ahead of the meeting in London of the Commonwealth heads of government in April 2018.

Even then, as the scandal hit the front pages, it remained survivable for then Home Secretary Amber Rudd – she had merely been implementing the policies brought in by her predecessor. But then she made the classic mistake: either by going in front of MPs underbriefed, or through a simple misstatement, she denied that the Home Office had targets for removals. After failing to tamp down the scandal with a rapid and full retraction of her statement, Rudd was brought down once it became clear she had indeed been aware of – and had even written to the Prime Minister about – such targets.

Working out what really happens in such departments

is rare, as few people talk in the middle of such crises, and during them people are often most interested in protecting themselves or their minister – but it is possible to talk through after the fact how such events unfold in general terms.

Someone who has extensive first-hand experience in the Home Office is Jane Furniss CBE, a former senior civil servant who went on to lead the Independent Police Complaints Commission and who now sits on the board of the National Crime Agency. She set out in an interview how such crises could come about as a result of how the department recruits, recognises and promotes talent. Furniss noted that in the 'core' departments, such as the Home Office, Treasury, Foreign Office and others, promotion would generally come as a result of hopping from policy area to policy area – leading to ingrained short-termism in what is supposed to be the long-term bureaucracy supporting government.

'You may not have to move physically, but moving areas to know a wide range and practise your skills in those different subjects is seen as necessary and to be encouraged,' she said.

The danger of that is very often people don't see the damaging consequences or the benefits of what they did, because they're no longer in that subject area when the shit hits the fan, or the success arrives ...

That has real consequences for how people learn about the consequences of the work they do. The recent Windrush debacle highlights that: the architects of the hostile environment policy are probably no longer in that area of work at all, and even if they were warned of consequences, they will have been focused on delivering the policy – they won't be there when it comes home.

She said that these kinds of backlashes aren't infrequent – they're an ingrained part of the system: because the top of the civil service is structured around supporting ministers, prestige is found in moving around as what ministers want changes, rather than sticking with a specialism. Nor is this an accident: high-level dilettantism is government policy, and has been for many decades. Giving evidence to Parliament in May 2018, Oliver Dowden, Minister for the Cabinet Office, enthusiastically confirmed that he wanted Permanent Secretaries to be hired for their leadership skills, not their subject knowledge.

'I think it is a combination of the leadership skills, which is more of a generalist thing, and the subject knowledge,' he told a parliamentary select committee, after being asked if he favoured generalists over specialists. 'I do not think it is always the case that subject knowledge trumps everything else.'

Furniss expands on this idea – explaining that people are moved around so often that they're often not there when consequences kick in. 'All sorts of time I'd see people work on huge policy areas that were a priority for ministers – Police and Crime Commissioners, or crime prevention, and so on – none of the people who worked on that policy and the legislation that underpinned it, or those authorities, are anywhere near it now,' she said. 'The corporate memory and the analysis of "Did it work?", they're not asked those questions.'

The bluffers have moved on somewhere else. So have the ministers. So have the journalists covering that beat.

Furniss concluded that the civil service's approach

of prizing cleverness and flexibility above all else built a different culture than other public services, such as the police or the NHS. 'These do attract people who are not wedded to a particular skill, service or policy area – contrast it with the cops; many more people in the police and health service commit to their role for life,' she concludes. 'In the civil service you get heavily involved in depth into a narrow area, then you drop it and move to another one. I think that does appeal to a different kind of person to the person who works steadily away in one field.'

Because what is most valued is what directly supports and advises ministers – especially if it gets them out of a crisis – management and other skills fall lower down the pecking order. Someone in the Border Agency could manage 500 staff and a large budget but not be counted as senior civil service, whereas someone managing virtually no staff and no budget but writing policy papers may enjoy much higher internal status. The same hierarchy applies to tax, welfare and defence. And, crucially, if something goes wrong for a staffer in an operational agency like the Border Agency, they 'will never, ever meet the Home Secretary', Furniss notes. 'Someone else will brief her, while they will be getting the blame for it.'

Overall, across government, even the most senior specialist officials get sidelined from the most senior grades of the structure. In some departments, they are stuffed into 'Grade 4', in civil service parlance, a rank which is technically in the top flight but which rarely leads to further promotion. Grade 4 is the loose sock drawer of the senior civil service; a place to put those who have essential brains but lack the faces that fit. 'People like the chief medical officer, significant experts in their fields – chief scientist, too – researchers, scientists, medics, lawyers, are all very often Grade 4-type roles,' Furniss says. 'Because that's the only way they can categorise them, and it takes them out of the ladder – and very, very few of those people get back onto the ladder up to the next grade again.'

The culture of the civil service still under-rewards management, handholds unwitting specialists into peripheral advisory roles, struggles to hire large numbers of graduates with science and technological backgrounds, and contributes to the short-termism that fuels many of the policies which then backlash, either against those they are intended to help or against the ministers in charge of implementing them – or both.[17]

❊   ❊   ❊

The structure of the UK civil service is quite particular to the country – few other places have managed to pick up all of its quirks – but other aspects of government that favour bluffers are more internationally standard. One such trait is ministerial amateurism, which sees huge swathes of the UK left in the hands of people with no experience of that sector. The average tenure of a UK Cabinet minister is around two years and four months – but many have moved around far more rapidly.

Take Sajid Javid, who joined Parliament after a career in the City. Within an eighteen-month period, he was shifted from a role as City minister – a role clearly suited to his expertise – to Minister for Equalities, to

---

17  Most of these criticisms appear in the Fulton Report, a wide-ranging review of the civil service that took place in the 1960s. The review's recommendations were largely neutered by Whitehall.

Secretary of State for Culture, Media and Sport, before being shifted back to a role he would appear more obviously qualified for: Business Secretary. Qualification was not, of course, enough to save Javid from politics. When Theresa May became Prime Minister following Brexit, Javid was demoted to the role of Housing, Communities and Local Government Secretary – only to be promoted up to Home Secretary (despite never having worked in criminal justice) to defuse a political scandal.[18]

That's six different roles within the space of four years, the longest of which lasted twenty-one months, the shortest of which a mere three. Each shift is months of on-the-job learning, as well as disruption to the special advisors and ministerial priorities and other upheavals. Plus, when everyone concerned knows shifts will be based on simple politics, there is even less focus on the long term than there otherwise would be.

Another problem the UK shares with many other countries, though by no means all, is the limited pool

---

18 Javid, incidentally, is notorious in Whitehall for giving the impression that he believes most civil servants are crap, possibly because they are less brazenly confident at bluffing than his old colleagues in the City.

from which it draws. While few would sing the praises of the expertise of Donald Trump's Cabinet, the US system is far more open to outside experts taking roles. US Cabinet Secretaries are not drawn from Congress, making it far easier to hire lifelong experts in their field to run departments: foreign policy roles can draw from top academic international relations projects, for example. The system also, generally at least, leads to longer tenures: the average US Cabinet Secretary works for around a year longer than their UK counterpart.

Beyond these issues lies a once-in-a-generation political crisis of confidence: the loss of trust in mainstream politics, and a corresponding rise in populism and support for anti-establishment views. Elsewhere across Europe this has directly manifested itself in surging support for far-right parties – Marine Le Pen finished second in the French presidential race, while the far-right AfD party polled close to 15 per cent in the German elections.

For a variety of reasons, including the first-past-the-post electoral system, the UK has not seen a similar surge in direct support for far-right parties – aside from the extremist and anti-Muslim 'Britain First' party, which became the largest UK party on Facebook with two million likes, despite having zero elected officials.

The obvious manifestation of anti-elite sentiment in the UK, though, is Brexit: despite the overwhelming majority of elite opinion, plus that of the leaders from the three biggest political parties, the country narrowly voted to leave – after a slickly produced but shallow and largely dishonest campaign which focused little on the realities of leaving the EU, instead promising £350 million a week extra funding for the NHS, supposedly from money saved on EU payments.[19] Elsewhere, the campaign suggested Turkey was on the verge of joining the EU, among other highly questionable statements.

These promises were rebutted by the official UK statistical watchdog, by independent fact checkers, by frontbench politicians, and by huge swathes of the mainstream media, including the BBC. Why, then, did it still connect so well with so many millions of voters? If we're

---

19 This topic is tackled at length in Chapter Two of *Post-Truth: How Bullshit Conquered the World*. (*Utterly shameless plug here from James – AG*)

honest, we'll never have a definitive answer, but it certainly can't have helped that the Remain campaign was somewhat out of touch, or that the referendum campaign came a decade into a pay freeze for the nation, and six years into austerity.

But it also cannot have helped that the public had got endlessly used to hearing the in-game-focused language of the bluffer coming from politicians, the media and lots of the think tanks and expert bodies, too. After years of having to parse the intellectual non-denial denials, evasions and rhetorical tricks that come with the bluffocracy, the public could easily be forgiven for having had enough, for losing trust in all concerned.

Politics still works in an outdated form of communications, where the principle of collective Cabinet responsibility – that all ministers must be bound by all decisions made by the Cabinet – has been pushed to an unrealistic extent. In the modern era, virtually anything any politician has ever said can be looked up by anyone with an internet connection in just minutes, whether uttered in the chamber or in any TV or radio appearance.

And yet politicians are still expected to go out and earnestly defend a policy which there is years of evidence that they either never really supported or even actively opposed. Briefed by their advisors, or by No. 10, they dodge questions about their previous opinions and listlessly detail the merits of the policy. The interviewer knows full well they're talking nonsense, the person speaking knows they're talking nonsense – and a reasonable chunk of the audience will quickly work out they're talking nonsense. This is a tired ritual that has no need to continue: why should the public trust politicians when the rules of public life require them to speak dishonestly almost daily? Who benefits from this endless ritual – and would the British political system really collapse if a minister said, 'I didn't fully agree with this policy, but couldn't persuade enough of my Cabinet colleagues of my view, and I'm happy to go with their wisdom on this issue. It's worth it for all the other excellent work this government is doing'?

*　*　*

We could, if we wanted, go much further than just dropping the unwritten requirement for ministers to routinely dissemble on television. One start when we're thinking about the media is to look at what could happen if we dropped the lobby system, or at least if a few outlets working in concert dropped out of it: provided they had audiences some politicians felt they needed to reach, such a move could spell the beginning of the end of the closed shop.

The possibilities this could generate are promising: it needn't mean scrapping the idea of specialist political reporters who know who's up and who's down, or the details of parliamentary procedure and the nuances of different language changes.

But it opens up a new range of coverage and accountability: the journalist who has spent time travelling the country meeting people affected by stricter benefit sanctions is far less likely to get fobbed off on that issue than someone who's never seen the enforcement in action. The same is true of specialist immigration or health reporters – they don't get zero access to ministers now, but having them able to attend daily No. 10

briefings and similar huddles would mean a better level of policy scrutiny, and help them put policy rather than politics onto the front page.

Elsewhere, commentators could try to be more aware of when they[20] reverse position or make a prediction that's totally wrong – there could even be space to note and explain this towards the bottom of new pieces, where it's significant. Some writers do this now, but it's far from the norm. Trying to predict what's happening next, especially in modern politics, is extremely difficult, so it's no sin for writers to make the wrong calls. Where it turns into bluffing, and something corrosive to trust, is the constant overconfidence: never mind that I was wrong four times out of the last five, believe my absolute certainty this time. If newspapers wanted to be really radical, they could consult with their specialist reporters and commentators before they get a 24-year-old to write the paper's official position on matters of national and international policy.

For the civil service, the right answer, typically

---

20 OK, 'we'.

enough, is probably a slower burn. Given that it is 160 years since the bureaucracy had a genuinely comprehensive review of what it gets up to and whether it is appropriately arranged for the modern world, one could argue such an examination might be a little overdue. For any civil service reforms to have a hope of succeeding, they need to be led by a powerful minister in charge of a powerful department. A new Gladstonian figure taking on the agenda from the Treasury would be nice. But since such political figures are thin on the ground, and because that course of action is bound to lead to much shrieking without immediate political benefit for any government brave enough to take it on, radicalism is unlikely to get far without a particularly special set of circumstances. If history is any guide, a decent-sized war is probably the only reliable way of moving the needle. That said, neither of us would advocate for armed conflict solely to cure Whitehall's ills, which is why we wouldn't thrive on talk radio.[21]

Better to start small, then. Plenty of good work does

---

21 Well, probably. If any stations would like to try us out, do get in touch.

actually happen in government, believe it or not. Invaria-
bly, the best of it is done by teams made up of a variety of
skills – policy, economics, science, user research, design,
technology – who focus relentlessly on what citizens
need, rather than what government needs. Ignoring
Whitehall's own siloes – the internecine squabbling
between departments and the quiet turf wars between
different professions – is essential. Bluffers' skills will
still be needed in those teams, but they should be diluted
and complemented by experts in a range of other fields.
Having a senior generalist in London toss policy over
the wall to a bemused delivery office in Warrington
should become a thing of the past. Ministers will get
better advice as a result.

Giving Whitehall the motivation to do this will mean
making sure civil servants get asked a higher quality of
difficult questions by the people employed to do so.
Senior officials are usually terrified about two things:
appearing in front of parliamentary committees, and the
*Daily Mail*. There's not much you can do about the latter, but the former is an under-explored lever for change.
The people supposed to hold senior civil servants to

account – select committees, regulators, the National Audit Office – are always short of resources and time. Beef up the teams who support the UK's democratic accountability mechanisms with more scientists, designers, developers and ex-public servants who know where the bodies are buried. Ask questions that are designed to force specialists to turn up and explain the answers, rather than encouraging pat responses from bluffers who are exquisitely skilled in defusing barbed enquiry. Better yet, hold teams of officials to account from the start of a policy, rather than picking through the wreckage afterwards. Civil servants will raise their game to keep up.

These steps mark only small fixes, and yet even these seem vanishingly unlikely, and difficult to even begin in our institutions as they are. That's because, as we flagged in the early parts of this essay, bluffers aren't built when they join any of the three institutions we highlight, but before it – through our education system and through the courses and skills we value there.

This isn't about trying to change one of our institutions all at once, but instead recognising that we've created a feedback loop that rewards the generalist over the specialist, the quick thinker over the deep thinker, and the bright idea over the diligent implementation. Ambitious people hoping to attend university look to those at the top of public institutions and apply for courses with that in mind.

People tend to hire and promote others like them, and so the institutional values remain geared towards the soft skills upon which we've focused. Rather than trying to make a change in isolation, we need to try to change each a little all at once – the kind of slow and gradual change unappealing to bluffers like us, but one that could in time make a real difference to the type of country we live in.

# Coda

FACED WITH THE prospect of taking part in a public panel discussion, needing to give a ten-minute speech followed by discussion, there are two types of people in British public life.[22] One sort will immediately jump into research mode: looking up the title of the panel, its intended audience, the other speakers and their interests, before writing a rough draft of their speech and noting a few key figures that might be useful as answers to questions. The other sort might scribble down ten words as notes in the back of the cab on the way to the event.

British public life, by and large, has far too many of the latter – and it's time to redress the balance.

---

22 There is a third type of person, who would never agree to do such a thing in the first place, but they tend to be very rare in this part of the world.

We should note that we haven't in our argument intended to battle a straw man, and we don't want to create one, either. Token attempts to bring 'businessmen' into politics, on either side of the Atlantic, have often failed. Soft skills have value, as do rhetoric and quick analysis.

We are not saying every person, or even every bluffer – the people like us – in public life should vanish from the scene. What we *are* saying is that this is a question of balance, and it's our view that in the UK the balance has shifted far too much in the favour of the generalist and against the specialist, to the real detriment of us all. Bluffers have a lot to offer. They should be part of the team. They shouldn't be the whole team.

If we can learn to really bring experts into public debate, rather than simply using them as tools to support a rhetorical point or justify a policy, we can engage better with new ideas without having to wait for them to go wrong in the real world. If we can learn to value people – specialist and generalist alike – who might not have the bluffer trick of faking knowledge, but who can genuinely, if quietly, bring insight to the table, we will do much better.

If we can shift away from prizing traits which are tilted to favour (though of course not without exceptions) the privately educated over the state schooled, the Oxbridge grad over the Russell Group, the men over the women, and more, we will build a more diverse and thus more robust public policy machine, making our government and media more reflective of our society, and hopefully improving policy, too.

The UK is no longer running on autopilot. After 29 March 2019, things will change markedly, whether we support those changes or not. The world stage is fluid and, as we are often reminded, we are on the cusp of a new technological revolution – the rise of artificial intelligence – which could potentially be the largest since the industrial revolution itself.

If Britain leaves its current crop of people who habitually wing it at the helm, we could be in for an especially rocky thirty years ahead. But if we can find ways to bring in expertise, to reform how the courses that educate our elite operate, to change how career progression works, and to reshape our media so as not to punish people for trying to give honest and nuanced answers based on expertise, rather than bluffing on through, we can do better.

The first step can be a tiny one, especially for self-confessed bluffers like the authors of this book. It could be as simple as learning a new three-word phrase, and using it whenever the urge to blag strikes.

'I don't know.'

# About the authors

**James Ball** has worked in political, data and investigative journalism in the US and UK for BuzzFeed, *The Guardian* and the *Washington Post* in a career spanning TV, digital, print and alternative media. His reporting has won the Pulitzer Prize for public service and the British Journalism Award for investigative reporting, among others. He wrote *Post-Truth: How Bullshit Conquered the World* (Biteback, 2017) and has co-authored two other books: *WikiLeaks: News in the Networked Era* and *The Infographic History of the World*.

**Andrew Greenway** is a former government official who worked in five UK central government departments before reaching the senior civil service at twenty-seven. He left the bureaucracy in 2014, and now works as a partner for Public Digital, advising governments and large organisations around the world on institutional reform. He has written on politics and Whitehall for *The Guardian*, the *New Statesman* and *Civil Service World*. This is his second book *(He doesn't want to name the first one – JB)*.